IN THE SHADE OF THE TREE

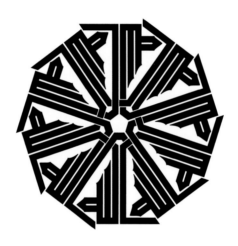

IN THE SHADE OF THE TREE

A Photographic Odyssey Through the Muslim World

PETER SANDERS

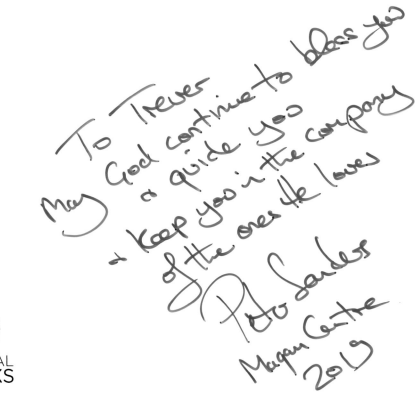

To Trevor

May God continue to bless you
& guide you
& keep you in the company
of the ones He loves

Peter Sanders
Maqam Centre
2019

INSPIRAL
BOOKS

PHOTOGRAPHY
Peter Sanders

DESIGN & LAYOUT
Ian Whiteman

PRODUCTION MANAGER
Muhammad al Mukhtar Sanders

PROOFREADER
Muhammed Isa Waley

COLOUR SEPARATIONS
Bayeux, London, UK

PRINTING
Mega Basim, Istanbul, Turkey

FIRST EDITION JOINTLY PUBLISHED BY
STARLATCH PRESS USA & MOUNTAIN OF LIGHT UK
Copyright © 2002 by Peter Sanders
Starlatch Press (USA) ISBN: 1-929-694-14-8
Mountain of Light (UK) ISBN: 1-900-675-41-2

SECOND EDITION PUBLISHED BY INSPIRAL BOOKS
24 Meades Lane, Chesham, Bucks, HP5 1ND, UK
website: www.inspiralbooks.com
e-mail: info@inspiralbooks.com
Copyright © 2007 by Peter Sanders
ISBN-13: 978-0-9557106-0-5

British Library Cataloging-in-Publication Data
A catalogue record for this book is available from the British library

PREFACE

In the Shade of the Tree is the result of many years of painstaking observation of shade. The word photographer literally means "one who writes with light." The photographer of this volume has been "capturing shade" for decades. Shade is a sign of God. The Quran says: "Have you not considered your Lord, how He extends the shade, and had He willed He would have made it still? Then We made the sun its guide, then We withdraw it unto Us gradually." Shade is an admixture of light and darkness. The cosmos is a shadow of the Reality, and Peter Sanders has spent a lifetime reflecting on it. If beauty is in the eye of the beholder, then these pictures are a testimony to the beauty in Sanders' eye. He uses an odd yet wondrous mechanical device that captures for one brief moment a glimpse of beauty. The pictures in this book, while only brief moments of shade written in light captured by his discerning eye, will linger on in your memory long after you have closed the book.

HAMZA YUSUF

All the major traditions confirm the
temporary nature of this life.

Describing himself in relation to the world,
the Prophet Muḥammad said,

I am in this world like a traveller who
takes shade under a tree, only to resume his journey.

The idea of this book and its accompanying exhibition
developed after reading the above tradition. As we
shade under our own trees—large or small—we
reflect on moments and events in our lives. This book
of photographs, taken at an average shutter speed
of 1/125th of a second, does not even amount to one
half of one second of worldly time, but will remain as
treasured moments for many years to come.

Peter Sanders

DOORWAY OF MYSTERY

There was a door to which I found no key,
there was a veil past which I could not see.

ʿUmar Khayyām

PAINTED DOOR IN THE OLD WALL

RABAT, MOROCCO

Rabat is a wonderful city, although I hadn't always thought so. It
wasn't until I spent some time working there that I discovered its
hidden beauty. I especially love the old wall that surrounds the
city, and it was during an exploration of the wall that I discovered
a series of old doors. This one captivated me the most.

A MOMENT IN OR OUT OF TIME

A day with your Lord is as a thousand years
of what you reckon.

The Quran, 22:47

The old wall of Rabat holds a particular fascination for me. I sat
in a café as the sun began its descent. I used the gate as stage
left and the lamp post as stage right. I then waited. Eventually a
man in traditional attire entered the setting. I knew then what I
had been waiting for. The picture relates a sense of timelessness.

A PINK ROOM IN A MUD PALACE

Noah said, "My Lord, forgive me and my parents
and whoever enters my household a believer,
and all believing men and women."

The Quran, 71:28

QALʿAT AL-MAGŪNAH
SOUTH MOROCCO

On a journey through Morocco in the early 1970s, I was invited to
a meal in a mud palace in Qalʿat al-Magūnah, a rose-growing region
in the northern Sahara just south of the High Atlas. The craftsmen
would sing praises of God while building these homes. The room is
a striking pink as the photo shows, with hand-woven carpets lining
the floor. The wall and ceiling designs were all painted by Imām
Mūlay Ḥasan, pictured here with his son.

THE JOURNEY

The journey of the pilgrim is two steps and no more.
One is transcending beyond selfhood
and the other is toward nearness with the Friend.

Maḥmūd Shabistarī

THE SAHLIJ SCHOOL
FEZ, MOROCCO

During a recent visit to the old city of Fez, I was introduced to
this historic religious college. In visiting such a place, one may
suddenly receive a distinct flavour of the distant past. At one
time, these schools were full of vigorous students, living in
small rooms, praying and studying like bees in a hive, gathering
the nectar known as "knowledge of God."

COURT OF LIONS

These are our traces that we leave behind.
They indicate who we were.
So look, after we are gone, at our traces.

Andalusian Poem

I made a trip to document Andalusian Spain, which, of course, had to include the spectacular Muslim palace in Granada known as "Alhambra." It is constantly full of visitors these days, so an enormous amount of patience is necessary when attempting to capture on film a glimpse of the majestic past. As the afternoon progresses, the Court of Lions goes through extraordinary changes of light.

GARDENS OF ANDALUSIA

Indeed, the righteous will be amid gardens
and fountains.

The Quran, 15:45

GARDEN OF REFUGE (GENERALIFE)

ALHAMBRA PALACE

GRANADA, SPAIN

Spending hours in the gardens of Alhambra Palace trying to capture
the spirit of the place in a photograph felt like therapy. The sound
of running water, the songs of birds, the variety of colours,
the setting sun, and the subtle stillness of it all would cause the
insane to become sane and the sane to taste ecstasy.

A GIRL IN GREEN

So be patient, with a beautiful patience!

The Quran, 70:5

Drawn to a newly built mosque by the ocean, I became aware
of this young girl collecting water for its visitors. As I looked
through the lens and studied her face more closely, it occurred to
me that she was suffering from malaria, which is not uncommon
in West Africa. But through the transparency of her illness, I saw
also an inner beauty that emanated from remarkable patience.

WONDERING WHAT THE FUTURE HOLDS

Reflect upon the beauty of the creation on land and sea.
Look into God's attributes both openly and secretly.
In the self and on the horizon is the greatest witness
to God's perfections, which are limitless.

Shaykh Muḥammad ibn al-Ḥabīb

SUMBUJUN BEACH
DAKAR, SENEGAL
WEST AFRICA

In Senegal, a country of mostly poor but happy people, there is hardly
a single moment in which one does not hear the Quran recited, a song
sung, or the beat of music. On Sumbujun beach, famous for fishing, I
noticed these two boys gazing out to sea, perhaps contemplating their
future, dressed in the robes of circumcision.

DESERT SOLITUDE

That serene place belongs to the one occupied
with the correction of his own self
who struggles against it in every state.

Shaykh Muḥammad ibn al-Ḥabīb

THE DESERT OF MAURITANIA
SAHARAN AFRICA

We spent three days and nights in this remote place in the
desert—nights in which the winds blew and covered us with a
thin layer of sand. Meanwhile, Shaykh ʿAbd al-Rahmān prayed.

IN THE SHADE OF THE TREE

Have you not considered your Lord, how He extends the shade, and had He willed He would have made it still? Then We make the sun its guide, then We withdraw it unto Us gradually.

The Quran, 25:45–46

LAHSIRA, MAURITANIA

In the desert, anything that offers shade is a blessing and is greatly appreciated. Every tree in the desert of Mauritania is a unique sculpture.

THE INVISIBLE THREAD LINKING
STUDENT AND TEACHER

Indeed, the angels lower their wings for the seeker
of sacred knowledge, pleased with what he is doing.
The creatures in the heavens and the earth seek
forgiveness for the student of sacred knowledge,
even the fish in the sea.

Prophet Muḥammad ﷺ

On a journey deep into the Mauritanian desert, I was brought
into the presence of this great teacher. He sleeps little, eats
little, and spends his days serving his students. The students
study hard all day every day. Their relaxed postures here are
not regarded as impolite but are a means of helping them to
maintain concentration during long periods of continuous study.

THE WEALTH OF POVERTY

The scholars are the heirs of the prophets.
The prophets leave no money as a bequest.
Rather, they leave knowledge.
Whoever seizes it has taken a bountiful share indeed.

Prophet Muḥammad ﷺ

The students of Twemerit are full of light and are not trapped by the material world. I asked the one on the left to pose for me. Self-conscious about his shaven head, he was shy and reluctant. I assured him that it made him look noble. He eventually agreed as long as I included his friend. They carry their writing boards with them wherever they go, using every spare moment to learn whatever they are studying, whether it is the Quran, Sacred Law, or any of the other Islamic sciences.

INSTANT WISDOM

A man's wisdom makes his face to shine.

Ecclesiastes, 8:1

THE DESERT OF MAURITANIA
SAHARAN AFRICA

The qualities of timelessness and concentration enable the
desert children to play for hours with such things as a small
piece of sheep's fur. There are no computers or television,
in fact, no electricity. When I once again met this boy, now
matured into a young man, I noted that there was still no beard,
though a certain nobility and wisdom was growing in his heart.

THE MASTER OF THE TIMES

What good is an increase in wealth when life grows ever shorter? So be joyous only for an increase in knowledge or in good works, for they are your two companions that will accompany you in the grave when your family, wealth, children, and friends stay behind.

Imām Abū Ḥāmid al-Ghazālī

THE DESERT OF MAURITANIA

SAHARAN AFRICA

A memorizer of the entire Quran, Shaykh Muḥammad ʿAlī is known also as the Master of the Times. This title is given to special people who are able to tell when the time of any of the five daily prayers has arrived, without the aid of any device other than a stick and the length of its shadow. He can also tell which day it is by the movement of the stars. He has a very lovable personality, and one feels strongly drawn to his company.

THE LIGHT OF KNOWLEDGE

The pleasure of life is only in the company of the *fuqarā'*,
who have recognized their utter dependence on God.
They are the true sultans, masters, and princes.

Shaykh Abū Madyan

After driving for many hours through the Mauritanian desert,
we arrived at the tent of this great scholar, Shaykh Aḥmad Fāl, a
completely unpretentious gentleman who sat surrounded by his
books. He was a gracious host. As our visit concluded, we asked
if there was anything he needed. After a moment, his reply was:
"Just a small mud building to protect my books. Every time
there is a sand-storm, my books are ruined!"

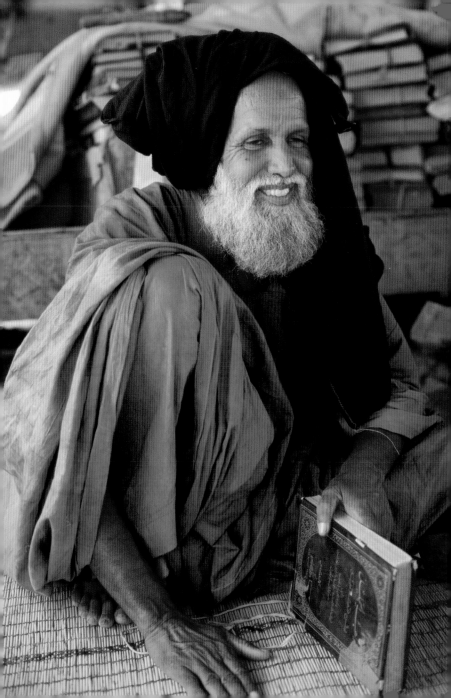

THE BEST BIRTHDAY PARTY
IN THE WORLD

Take delight in hearing of his good character,
and speak of his noble qualities.

Shaykh Muḥammad ibn al-Ḥabīb

SMALL BOYS CELEBRATING THE BIRTHDAY
OF THE PROPHET MUḤAMMAD ﷺ
LAMU ISLAND, KENYA
EAST AFRICA

I had wanted to visit the Island of Lamu since the early 1970s,
when a Dutch painter had described it to me as "paradise on earth."
There are no cars on the island except one, belonging to the District
Commissioner, and no roads except one, the one running from the
District Commissioner's house to his office. I had the good fortune
to be there during the celebrations of the birthday of the Prophet
Muḥammad ﷺ, a joyous time. I was amazed by the purity and beauty of
the people. After the Friday Prayer, the elders of the community lead a
procession through the old streets of Lamu, reciting prayers as they walk
along. They end up at the tomb of the great spiritual sage of the island,
Ḥabīb Sahlī, and there they sit, in vast numbers, with their banners
flapping in the cool sea breezes, supplicating to God.

CATCH THE MOMENT

The world is but a moment,
so make it a moment of obedience.

Imām al-Shāfiʿī

LAMU ISLAND, KENYA

EAST AFRICA

During the Quran recitation competition, featured at the end
of the celebration of the Prophet's birthday on the Island of
Lamu, I found these three girls in front of me. When I lifted the
camera to my eyes and began focusing, the girls had adopted this
great pose. I would love to know what they were saying.

THE PLAY OF WATER, LIGHT, AND FRIENDSHIP

A friend is not a true friend unless
he protects his friend in three situations:
in his misfortune,
in his absence,
and at his death.

Caliph and Imām ʿAlī ibn Abī Ṭālib ﷺ

TUTTI ISLAND

KHARTOUM, SUDAN

Near the end of my journey in Sudan, the Sudanese government decided to put me up in the Khartoum Hilton. High up in my room, I had a spectacular view of the Nile. One day, I saw children washing horses in the river, so I grabbed my cameras and ran down to them. By the time I reached the other side of the river via the ferry, they had disappeared. However, just before sunset that evening, I noticed these two girls hand in hand, playing, silhouetted against the river. I felt very fortunate to have been able to capture this quiet sense of love and sisterhood.

SQUEEZING IN THE FRAME

God is beautiful and He loves beauty.

Prophet Muḥammad ﷺ

SCHOOLGIRLS OF MUNĀ SALĀMAT AL-DAʿWA SCHOOL

KHARTOUM, SUDAN

During my travels through Sudan, I was taken to the Munā Salāmat
al-Daʿwa School. I was completely won over by the vibrancy of the
school children and the amazing atmosphere within the school. I hope
I captured some of it in this portrait of the girls.

GOD IS MY PROTECTOR

The heart is made serene by His remembrance,
so that it is stilled from fear of anything in creation
and of poverty.

Shaykh Muḥammad ibn al-Ḥabīb

QURAN SCHOOL IN MWEHLI REFUGEE CAMP
DESERT OUTSIDE KHARTOUM, SUDAN

During the mid-1980s I toured many of the refugee camps in
Sudan at the time of the drought. This particular camp was
outside Khartoum (Sudan's capital), but it felt like the middle
of nowhere. It was full of nomads from the Darfur Region. After
seven years of drought, these noble people were truly suffering.
They had lost all their livestock and were forced to move from
their lands, ending up in this wasteland. There was immense
hardship. Aid was present but in very small amounts. Despite all
this, the education of the children was always maintained and
each camp had established its own Quran school.

TOMB OF A SPIRITUAL SAGE

It is God who gave you life,
then He will cause you to die,
then again He will give you life
in the Hereafter.

The Quran, 22:66

DESERT OUTSIDE KHARTOUM, SUDAN

During one of my early visits to Sudan, I was travelling to visit the Mwehli Refugee camp outside Khartoum. As we drove across the barren landscape I came across this unusual tomb. I called to the driver of the Jeep to stop. Despite the delay, the passengers waited patiently while I took a few pictures before climbing back in to proceed to the camp.

COMPANIONS

None of you is a true believer
until he loves for his brother
what he loves for himself.

Prophet Muḥammad ﷺ

When photographing the River Nile one evening, I looked
around and saw these three boys closely watching me. I noticed
each one was a different shade of brown, and when I asked them
their names, I was told, "Abū Bakr, ʿUmar, and ʿAlī," which
happen to be the names of three of the closest companions to
the Prophet Muḥammad ﷺ fourteen centuries ago.

THE PRAYING MAN

Remember Me, and I shall remember you.

The Quran, 2:152

I am always aware that good photographs are a gift from God and
none more than this one. On a visit to Egypt, I travelled south
through Luxor, to the small village of Gourna on the far side of
the Nile. As I left the traditional mosque designed by the well-
known architect Ḥasan Fathy, I glanced back and saw this image
of a Muslim praying. Inscribed on the wall is the simple divine
name of God in Arabic, "Allāh." I was immediately struck by the
simplicity of Islam. I took two frames, and this is one of them.
This particular picture suggests the solitude of the spiritual path.

THE ASPIRATION OF MAN

Hand over your affairs to the One who knows best,
for it is He who knows our hearts and their desires.

Shaykh Muḥammad ibn al-Ḥabīb

Sultanahmet Mosque is also known as the "Blue Mosque." While taking this picture, I was reflecting on how this spectacular building arose from the inspiration and vision of one man, Mehmet Ağa, a student of the great architect Sinān. It was at this moment that a worshipper stepped into my camera's frame and began supplicating God, giving the image scale, purpose, and much more meaning.

SUNSET OVER
AN ANCIENT LAND

His is the sovereignty of the heavens
and the earth, and to Him will all matters
return. He causes the night to pass into
the day and the day to pass into the night.

The Quran, 57:5–6

MINARET OF ARARAT

It was said, "Earth, swallow up your water!"
and "Heaven, hold back your rain!"
And the water subsided and the affair was concluded,
and the Ark came to land on al-Jūdī.

The Quran, 11:44

Mount Ararat, where traditionally Noah's Ark is believed to
have come to rest after the Flood, is an impressive landmark
on the Silk Route. But there is now archeological evidence of a
great sea vessel on Mount Jūdī, another mountain nearby,
which is mentioned in the Quranic passage above.

LIGHT AND SHADE

Without physical light,
we would not be able to define shades,
hues, and colours.
Without the divine aspect of light,
we would not be able to discern
between right and wrong.

I had waited thirty years to visit Iṣfahān, particularly the
Masjid-i Imām. Imagine my disappointment when I found
it under renovation. This narrowed my work to detail
rather than panoramic views. This picture suggests the
juxtapositioning of different worlds. I like the idea of a
hidden world woven with Arabic calligraphy.

THE ASPIRATIONS OF THE SCHOLAR

God took Muḥammad by night, after his mission had begun, to within two bows' length or nearer, until he achieved his heart's desire.

Shaykh Muḥammad ibn al-Ḥabīb

DOME OF THE ROCK JUST BEFORE SUNSET

JERUSALEM

Stairs have a visual fascination for me. I placed myself at the base of the stairs ascending to the Dome of the Rock itself. The light was slowly sinking and the mood was changing as I saw this scholar starting to climb the stairs in the shade on his way to the mosque to pray.

THE NOBLE SANCTUARY

Glory be to Him who took His servant, Muḥammad,
on a journey by night from the Sacred Mosque in
Makkah to the Furthest Mosque in Jerusalem,
whose surroundings We have blessed,
that We might show him some of Our signs.

The Quran, 17:1

Having photographed Makkah and Madīnah, I longed to
photograph Jerusalem to complete the three holy sites. This finally
happened in 1994 when a colleague working on a project about the
al-Aqṣā Mosque Complex invited me to accompany him. We were
given access to all the areas. I cannot begin to describe my awe in
exploring this historic site. The entire 36th chapter (Sura) of the
Quran is calligraphed around the top of the Dome of the Rock.
The blue of the sky with the blue of the stone is offset
by the faint moon appearing in the top left corner.

SHELTER FROM THE STORM

Make your concerns one,
and by Him all your needs will be met,
and you will enter into His protection.

Shaykh Muḥammad ibn al-Ḥabīb

AL-AQṢĀ MOSQUE
JERUSALEM

The al-Aqṣā Mosque Complex is deservedly known as the
"The Noble Sanctuary." Every morning while photographing
there, we would find Shaykh Muḥammad, who travelled daily
from a village some miles away, sitting and reading the
Quran from dawn until noon.

PRAISING THE ONE WORTHY OF PRAISE

Praise is due to You,
in number as great as the drops of rain,
the grains of sand, the pebbles,
the plants of the earth,
and the fish in the sea.

Shaykh Muḥammad ibn al-Ḥabīb

THE NAFŪD DESERT
KINGDOM OF SAUDI ARABIA

I love the desert. Although I had made many visits to Saudi Arabia,
I had never been to a desert with rich rolling dunes. When I was in
the region of Qasīm, someone offered to drive me into the Nafūd
Desert in the late afternoon, a favourite time for photography.
After about 60 kilometres, there we were among enormous sand
dunes. There are times in photography when images take on an
abstract nature, and as I looked into the landscape I began to see
Arabic calligraphy. The stillness and the purity of the moment was
soon disturbed, when a dune buggy appeared in my view-finder and
headed straight for me.

DISAPPEARING WORLDS

And We sent down from the sky water
in measured quantity, and We lodged it in the earth,
and We are well able to take it away. Then with it
We bring forth for you gardens of date-palms
and grapevines, in which there is abundant fruit
for you, from which you may eat.

The Quran, 23:18–19

NAJRĀN

KINGDOM OF SAUDI ARABIA

On my first visit to Najrān in Saudi Arabia, on the border with
Yemen, I had expected this oasis to be full of traditional houses.
Unfortunately, I had to search hard to find one that was not
damaged or about to collapse. Most of these beautiful houses are
now being replaced by modern breeze-block structures.

MINARET OF MĪQĀT MOSQUE

We have seen you turning your face toward the heaven.
We will surely turn you towards a direction
which will please you.

The Quran, 2:144

MADĪNAH THE ILLUMINATED

KINGDOM OF SAUDI ARABIA

I am full of appreciation for the mosques designed by
Abdul Wahid Wakeel, a student of the great and accomplished
architect Ḥasan Fathy. Abdul Wahid Wakeel renovated
Qiblatayn, Quba, and Miqat Mosque, and was responsible
for some of the new mosques along the Jeddah Corniche,
and many others worldwide. His simple soft lines play
with light and shadow, and this creates a wonderful
atmosphere within the buildings throughout the day.

RAMADAN MOON

And they ask you about the new moons.
Say, "They are a means for people to tell time
and to determine the Pilgrimage."

The Quran, 2:189

ROAD TO MAKKAH

KINGDOM OF SAUDI ARABIA

During a solitary drive from Madīnah to Jeddah early one
Ramadan morning, this spectacular coloured sky revealed itself
like a vision on the horizon.

THE *KISWA*

Abraham and Ishmael raised the foundation of
the House; they said, "Our Lord, accept this from us.
Indeed, You are the Hearing, the Knowing."

The Quran, 2:127

THE KAʿBA

MAKKAH THE NOBLE

KINGDOM OF SAUDI ARABIA

The black cloth or *kiswa*, embroidered with gold inscriptions,
veils the Kaʿba, the sacred building in Makkah that is considered
to be the geographical heart of Islam and the direction toward
which Muslims pray. Once a year, on the Day of ʿArafāt during
the Ḥajj, the black cloth is changed. This procedure takes most
of the day to complete, and at no point is the Kaʿba entirely
uncovered. It is performed very modestly, putting on the new
cloth while slipping off the old.

THE MYSTERY OF THE KAᶜBA

Likened to the believer's heart which he orbits
constantly, veiled from its interior, the mystery
continues to draw us like bees to nectar.

When you are near the Kaᶜba in Makkah, you feel that you are at the
heart of the world. Built by the Prophet Abraham ﷺ, the Kaᶜba is
illuminated by the light of the people who go around it. On my first
visit in 1971, I was immediately struck by its size. It completely filled
my vision. This gave me the idea for this particular image.

AN ANGEL'S VIEW

And We have made the House a place of assembly
for the people and a place of safety.

The Quran, 2:125

SANCTUARY OF THE KAʿBA

MAKKAH THE NOBLE

KINGDOM OF SAUDI ARABIA

On the eve of the Eid festival at the end of the month of
Ramadan, I found myself placed on one of the highest buildings
in Makkah. The Holy City was filled to the brim with
worshippers. The unbroken mass of people stretched as far as the
eye could see. When they finally prayed the Eid prayer just
after sunrise, they appeared like one body.

THE ILLUMINATED CITY

The full moon has risen over us.

From a song for the Prophet Muḥammad ﷺ
sung upon his arrival at Madīnah

THE MOSQUE OF THE PROPHET
MADĪNAH THE ILLUMINATED
KINGDOM OF SAUDI ARABIA

The Eid Prayer in Madīnah, a city 300 miles north of Makkah,
is a spectacular event in itself. Established in our high vantage
point from before dawn, we patiently waited while
the worshippers quietly gathered.

THE VISIT

All whose journeys end at the house of a generous host
get what they ask for, even their utmost desires.

Shaykh Muḥammad ibn al-Ḥabīb

THE OTTOMAN SECTION OF THE PROPHET'S MOSQUE
MADĪNAH THE ILLUMINATED
KINGDOM OF SAUDI ARABIA

This location, initially the humble house of the beloved Prophet
Muḥammad ☫, established as a mosque for more than 1400 years,
has undergone many changes. Some of the greatest changes have been
made in recent years, involving the work of craftsmen from many
nations. They include sliding domes and a vast and complex air-
conditioning system. At the heart of this now immense building lies
the old Ottoman section of the mosque with its distinct green dome
surrounded by its smaller silver irregular domes.

BENEATH THE CANOPY

By night you soared from sanctuary to sanctuary
just as the resplendent moon moves across the night sky
illuminating gloomy darkness.

From *Qaṣīdat al-Burda* (Poem of the Cloak) of Imām al-Būṣīrī

THE GREEN DOME AT NIGHT
THE PROPHET'S MOSQUE
MADĪNAH THE ILLUMINATED
KINGDOM OF SAUDI ARABIA

Beneath the canopy of the green dome lies the burial place of the
Prophet Muḥammad ﷺ, loved by Muslims the world over. Madīnah the
Illuminated holds a special place within the hearts of the believers.

HANDS OF LIGHT

When My servants ask you about Me, indeed I am near.
I answer the prayer of the asker when he prays to Me.

The Quran, 2:186

THE PROPHET'S MOSQUE
MADĪNAH THE ILLUMINATED
KINGDOM OF SAUDI ARABIA

One of my favourite places to photograph is inside the Prophet's
Mosque in Madīnah. I am extremely grateful for having been
allowed to photograph there on many occasions. You see such
extraordinary people from every ethnic background quietly
worshipping in the mosque. I am acutely aware of the problem
of imposing upon people's private moments, so I always try to be
as discreet as possible. This man was so lost in his prayer that
he did not notice me taking this photograph.

FACES OF MADĪNAH

A smile is charity.

Prophet Muḥammad ﷺ

While in Madīnah photographing the old city, I came across this traditional bakery run by smiling Egyptians who willingly posed for this photograph. Since the redevelopment of Madīnah, this bakery unfortunately has disappeared.

SHADOWS AND REFLECTIONS

The cosmos is naught but meanings set up in forms.
All those who realize this are the people of discernment.

Shaykh Muḥammad ibn al-Ḥabīb

CITY OF LIGHT

MADĪNAH THE ILLUMINATED

KINGDOM OF SAUDI ARABIA

The white marble of the piazza area offers a great mirror image
of the people who wander across it. What is extraordinary is the
way the shadows appear denser than the bodies. Can we always
be sure that what we see is what actually is?

DAYBREAK REVEALS ITS HIDDEN TREASURE

By the moon,
and the night as it recedes,
and the morning as it shines forth,
this is surely one of the greatest signs.

The Quran, 74:32–35

WĀDĪ ḤAḌRAMAWT

AL-ḤAJARAYN, SOUTH YEMEN

Sacrificing our sleep, we set off at 2:30AM in order to arrive at
al-Ḥajarayn in time for the dawn light. By moonlight, we found
our chosen position and waited. Each degree of light
brought forth hidden treasures.

HIDDEN WORLDS

Peace be upon the people
protected wherever they go.
Happy ones are they!
How perfect is that in which they exult!

Shaykh Muḥammad ibn al-Ḥabīb

Tarīm is the home of some of the greatest scholars I have been
fortunate to meet. Here I joined the students of Tarīm as
they greeted one another after the Friday Prayer. The unusual
coloured glass added to the special atmosphere.

VISIT TO A PROPHET

Prophet Hūd said, "O my people, worship God.
You do not have any God except Him.
Will you not be God-fearing?"

The Quran, 7:65

For five days we rested in tents in this ancient place,
the burial site of the Prophet Hūd ﷺ, a prophet of
ancient Arabia. At night the stars were so near
we felt as though we could touch them.

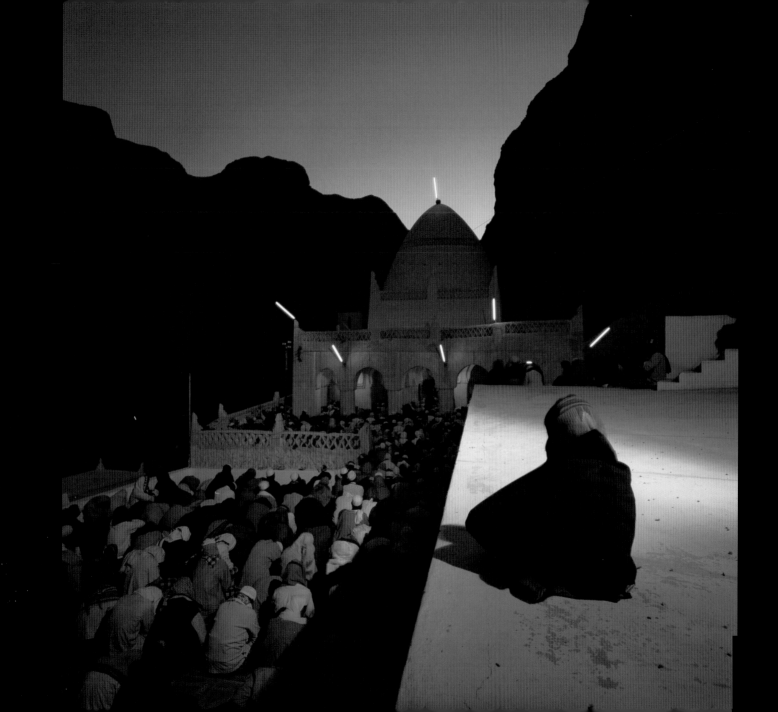

THE ENWRAPPED ONE

O you enwrapped in a cloak,
stay up at night, except a little,
half of it, a little less or a little more,
and recite the Quran distinctly.

The Quran, 73:1–4

THE VISIT TO THE PROPHET HŪD ﷺ

WĀDĪ ḤAḌRAMAWT

SOUTH YEMEN

The time between daybreak and sunrise is considered a special
time for prayer. While visiting the site of the Prophet Hūd ﷺ,
I saw this pilgrim completely absorbed in worship.

FARĪD–THE UNIQUE

It has been related that the first person whose hair turned white
was the Prophet Abraham ﷺ (the Friend of God).
Abraham asked, "O Lord! What is this?" His Lord answered,
"This is dignity." So Abraham said, "Lord, give me more dignity!"

Prophet Muḥammad ﷺ

Occasionally, people appear within my vision whom I am
irresistibly drawn to. Photographing in Tarīm, this
distinguished figure seemed to manifest in front of me.
I entered his presence and he allowed this intimate portrait
to be taken. After finishing and moving away, I turned back
and he had vanished, nowhere to be seen.

PINK GLASSES AT THE PINK BUS STOP

And among His signs is the creation of the heavens
and the earth and the variety of your tongues
and your colours. Surely in this are signs
for people of knowledge.

The Quran, 30:22

We had just crossed the border from Iran into Turkmenistan,
but not without difficulty. I was happy when I caught sight of
this imposing figure standing at a pink bus stop and wearing
pink glasses. I implored my colleagues to stop. We struck a deal:
in return for permission to photograph this man, we gave him a
ride to his destination. He looked quizzically at his new-found
travelling companions and then proceeded to praise God
non-stop for the rest of the journey.

PROVISIONS ON THE ROAD

The earth fulfilled her trust,
providing provisions,
by the permission of her Creator,
for creatures great and small.

From *Qaṣīdat al-Burda* (Poem of the Cloak) of Imām al-Būṣīrī

THE ROAD TO THE ANCIENT CITY OF MERV

TURKMENISTAN

CENTRAL ASIA

Along the Silk Route to the ancient city of Merv, once one of
the world's greatest cities, we stopped to purchase some apples
for our breakfast. It was with great dignity and modesty that
this Turkmen woman granted my request to photograph her.

THE CHILDREN OF THE SILK ROUTE

I love children. They are content with the least of
things, and gold and mud are the same in their eyes.

Prophet Muḥammad ﷺ

Travelling by land along the Silk Route, we entered
Turkmenistan and rested in the capital Ashgabat, which means
"Abounding in Love." Each evening as the intense heat of the
day eased, I would sit and talk to the local children playing
outside my hostel. Photographing them, I was able to
glimpse worlds within worlds.

THE WEDDING

He who marries secures half of his religion.

Prophet Muḥammad ﷺ

DISTRICT OF MERV

TURKMENISTAN

CENTRAL ASIA

My search for a traditional wedding in Turkmenistan took us on
a long drive through the outskirts of Merv (now called Mary).
Once we had permission, I was allowed into the house to set up
my equipment. I had assumed that I would be photographing only
the bride and groom, so imagine my surprise when this whole
entourage of women and children came
in and sat in front of me.

XIAN AND BEIJING'S OLDEST MOSQUES

Seek knowledge even in China.

Prophet Muḥammad ﷺ

[ABOVE] THE MOSQUE AT DAXUEXI LANE
XIAN, SHANXI PROVINCE, CHINA

This mosque is situated in "Big Learning Lane" established in
706 A.D. Muslims were in this ancient capital only 60 years after
the Prophet's migration to Madīnah. Within this building, I
found elements of a Zen monastery and feng shui, and yet it was
unmistakably a mosque.

[BELOW] NIUJIE MOSQUE
BEIJING, CHINA

Beijing's oldest mosque is over a thousand years old. Out of respect
for this beautiful building, it is constantly
cleaned, swept, and polished.

SERVICE AND STUDY

One does not acquire learning or profit from it,
unless one holds knowledge, and those who possess it,
in esteem.

Imām al-Zarnūjī

[ABOVE] IMĀM ḤAJJĪ YŪSUF
BAOQI, SHANXI PROVINCE, CHINA

I had longed to visit China since the 1970s. The meeting of
two great cultures was of great interest to me—Islam in China.
Twenty-five million Muslims is the unofficial figure. I finally
managed to travel there in the year 2000. For one hour, Ḥajjī
Yūsuf served us food and drink. For fifty years, though, he has
served his community as an Imām (religious teacher).

[BELOW] GIRLS' SCHOOL
HOHHOT, INNER MONGOLIA, CHINA

In a very humble dwelling, I found these young students
spending their days learning the Quran and studying Islam.

THE LIVES OF WOMEN

I am like a traveller who walks and then stops
and rests for a while in the shade of a tree,
then after sitting a while, continues on his way.

Prophet Muḥammad ﷺ

MUSLIM WOMEN

SHANXI PROVINCE AND INNER MONGOLIA, CHINA

The Lives of Man, a book by the great scholar of Ḥaḍramawt
Imām ʿAbdallāh al-Ḥaddād, examines the journey of the soul
through its different stages in this life and the next. From
this work, came the inspiration for this set of pictures.

TICK TOCK TO THE RHYTHM OF LIFE

All children are the beloved of God.

Prophet Muḥammad ﷺ

While visiting the ancient city of Xian, I was taken through the
narrow streets to visit a school for children aged from two to six.
For forty-five minutes they enthusiastically recited Quran, sang
songs, and utterly mesmerized me! The faces of these children

ACKNOWLEDGEMENTS

Islam teaches that as well as thanking the Creator we should also thank creation. I would therefore like to thank all my teachers who showed me so much patience, generosity, and compassion. I should also include all the people who appear in this book, as well as the thousands of others whom I have photographed over the years, for allowing me into their lives.

My gratitude is extended to Ateed Riaz without whose encouragement, constant support, and generosity, this project would never have begun. Ian Whiteman for his wonderful design. Muhammad al Mukhtar Sanders for his scrupulous attention to detail. Shaykh Hamza Yusuf for his invaluable help with some of the quotes and for occasionally carrying my camera bags. Starlatch Press for having the courage for seeing the process through to the end with the first edition. Finally to my wife Hafsa and the rest of my family for putting up with my long periods of absence.

For this second edition, it would not have been possible without our good friend Shezad Abedi's constant encouragement and help to reprint it. Also the devotion of Muhammad al Mukhtar Sanders to make this edition better than the first. Finally last but not least, Hafsa who is a living testament to multitasking.

BIBLIOGRAPHY

Qaṣīdat al-Burda (The Poem of the Cloak) by Imām al-Būṣīrī
Translated by Hamza Yusuf, Sandala Ltd, 2002

The Diwans of the Darqawa (Dīwān of Shaykh Muḥammad ibn al-Ḥabīb)
Translated by ʿAisha ʿAbd ar-Rahman at-Tarjumana, Diwan Press, 1980

Key to the The Garden by Ḥabīb Aḥmad Mashhūr al-Ḥaddād
Translated by Mostafa al-Badawi, Quilliam Press, 1990

Instruction of the Student: the Method of Learning by Imām al-Zarnūjī
Translated by G.E. Von Grunebaum & Theodora M. Abel, Starlatch Press, 2001

PETER SANDERS PHOTOGRAPHY WEB SITE: www.petersanders.com